LEADING
PRETEENS

LEADING
PRETEENS

PATRICK SNOW

Standard®
PUBLISHING
Bringing The Word to Life

Cincinnati, Ohio

Published by Standard Publishing, Cincinnati, Ohio
www.standardpub.com

Printed in the United States of America
Project editors: Heather Dunn, Elaina Meyers, Lu Ann Nickelson
Cover and interior design: Scott Ryan, Andrew Quach

ISBN 978-0-7847-2180-3

Library of Congress Cataloging-in-Publication Data

Snow, Patrick, 1977-
  Leading preteens / Patrick Snow.
     p. cm. -- (A growing ministry guide)
  ISBN 978-0-7847-2180-3 (perfect bound)
  1. Church work with preteens. 2. Christian education of preteens. I.
Title.

BV1475.9.S66 2007
259'.22--dc22

                          2007046629

13 12 11 10 09 08 07   9 8 7 6 5 4 3 2 1

DEDICATION

To Samantha, my partner in every part of life.
And to my parents who somehow lead four preteens
into faiths of their own.

ACKNOWLEDGEMENTS

The only way this book came to be was through the passion and hard work of Heather Dunn. Thank you, Heather, for taking the jumbled and sometimes incomprehensible ideas from my mind and somehow making sense of them. This book is as much yours as it is mine. I also would like to thank my good friend Eric Epperson. Many of the ideas and concepts in this book wouldn't exist if it weren't for the many discoveries we've made together over the last two years. Thanks for your partnership! Finally, I'd like to thank all the people who have helped shape our understanding of preteens: Teri Arnold, Matt Foreman, Jayson French, Katie Gerber, Andy Hansen, Chris Jefferson, Louie Murillo, Joe Puentes, Samantha Snow, and Craig Wilson.

CONTENTS

INTRODUCTION

An alarming new trend has begun to emerge in churches across America. Churches are experiencing a loss of students in the areas of 4th, 5th, and 6th grade. Preteen ministry is growing in response to this loss as many churches are beginning to realize that preteens are ready to move from children's ministry but aren't quite surviving their junior high programs. The harsh truth is that preteens don't fit into either children's or junior high ministry. Preteens need their own ministry. They need their own leaders and adult sponsors. They need to be taught the gospel of Christ in a way that is tailored just for them. The need for intentional preteen ministry is the first reason I got excited when the prospect of writing this book began.

In the last couple of years, I've had the privilege of leading an intentional preteen ministry called SuperStart! This weekend event provides a time and place where preteen students can experience worship, teaching, and small groups, all built around their specific learning and developmental needs. I can't even begin to describe to you how amazing it has been to see Jesus come alive in the life of someone who up until this point didn't even understand what a true relationship was.

But it hasn't always been amazing. That's the second reason I got excited about writing this book. When our SuperStart! team first began working on our event for preteens, we needed somewhere we could go that would help us understand preteens. Something that could explain how they tick, what they like, and, most importantly, how to best share the gospel of Jesus with them. We soon found out that any resources that came even remotely close to answering these questions were few and far between. And once we found those resources, we still had lots of questions.

We next turned to local church ministries who already had intentional preteen ministries. It was from those local church preteen ministries and a whole bunch of trial and error (I told you it hasn't always been amazing) that we finally began to figure out effective ways to communicate the Bible to preteens. But we've often wondered what those first years would have been like if there had been better resources to help us get our preteen ministry off the ground.

A lot of what is in this book are the questions and answers that our SuperStart! team has learned along the way—some from our own trials and errors, but most from the incredible local church ministries we've been blessed to partner with. Will this book answer every question you may have about leading preteens? Probably not. I'm still in the process of learning what's effective in sharing the gospel with preteens. But I do believe this book can effectively help your preteen ministry get a "super start"!

There is one more thing I want to say before we move on. Much of what you'll encounter in this book lands in the area of programming. From teaching to small groups to room decorating to event planning, it's all programming! And let's just call programming for what it is: a tool and nothing more. Too often I've been around ministries that rely on programs to change the lives of their students. Before you read this book, I want to remind you that the purpose of preteen ministry is to transform the lives of preteen students. Only an authentic encounter with the gospel of Christ and authentic relationships with adult leaders can bring about that transformation, not programming.

We, as leaders, need to keep our focus on Jesus too, making sure that everything else takes second place as we carry out our ministries.

As you can imagine, it's been an interesting process getting to understand how a preteen works. Which hopefully means this will be an interesting book. Let's find out!

—*Patrick Snow*

GET INTO
THEIR WORLD

What preteens are like and how to get to know them

The preteen world is always changing. Even if preteens describe it to me today, it'll be irrelevant by next year, maybe next month. News from yesterday is, well, yesterday. No matter how far away his friend lives, he's only a text second away. She knows the trends in fashion, talk, news, and stuff to own. I can't fool them or talk down to them. The preteen world is as complex and changing as mine. That's one thing I have in common with them for sure.

When I'm in staff meeting and the computer guy starts talking, I understand his first sentence or two. Then he starts explaining why we're having problems with this or that or why we're not going to be able to use the server, and I'm lost. I know he's talking about something really important to me and I want to understand, but try as I might, I don't get it. I can't track with his terminology. When he starts comparing two computer programs, it's way over my head. I completely check out when I don't know what he's saying. So I give up and gaze out the window. It's not out of disrespect; I totally think this guy is amazing. I think this

CHECK THIS OUT:
STATISTICS FOR KIDS AGES 6–11

37% eat breakfast with a parent daily
73% eat dinner with a parent daily
68% have some kind of TV rules
36% play sports of some kind
33% are in a club
32% take lessons of some kind
23% have changed schools
6% have repeated a grade
13% are in some sort of gifted class at school

is how our students feel sometimes. They love us and want to get what we're telling them, but we're speaking the wrong language and using the wrong examples.

DID I SAY LISTEN?

It takes more than Sunday mornings to get into their world. I watch some of their TV shows and listen to their songs. I listen to them when they talk to me and watch what they get excited about. I ask them about what sports they're in, what movies they're watching, and what video games they're playing. And I listen as we talk about issues in their families and with their friends. Did I say listen to them?

Getting into their world doesn't mean you have to act like them or pretend to like everything they do. But it does mean if you know a lot about them, you can help them navigate their choices and opportunities. It means you can use examples from their world to make your lessons relevant. The more you get into their world, the more you'll understand their thinking, and the more you'll be able to predict what'll work with them and what won't.

Observe or read about other ministries too, but don't copy them. For lots of reasons, don't try to be like other preteen ministries, no matter how cool or relevant they seem to be. God didn't give me anyone else's ministry, He gave me mine. The same is true for you. That means I'm supposed to minister to my unique group of preteens, and you're to minister to your group of preteens.

What's relevant or interesting to another group of preteens may not be relevant or interesting to mine. The preteens I'm supposed to be reaching may not be interested in someone else's video game-driven ministry. The students I'm supposed to reach may be drawn more to sports, music, or service projects. When I get into their world I'll know more what my students need. Now that doesn't mean I should ignore other successful ministries or shouldn't learn from them. Not at all. Look around—lots! I've gotten great ideas and insights from other ministries. But don't try to be just like them. Have the ministry with your students that God wants you to have. To find some information about preteen ministries, search the Internet for preteen ministries or preteen ministry blogs, and start asking around. There are some great ministries out there that'll give you fantastic ideas. You can also check out the SuperStart! event Web site at www.ciy.com/superstart.

USE THEIR WORLD STUFF

Use their preteen-world stuff to teach! Use examples from their world in every lesson. That's what Jesus did. Jesus used figs and coins and sheep—stuff His listeners could relate to, stuff from their world. Think of preteen-world examples ahead of time to use, stuff that your students can relate to. Use examples from video games, music, entertainment, family, school, sports, and friends. Ask your students to give you examples during the lesson too. When you use stuff from their world, your preteens will feel as though you understand them.

- being let down by someone
- making a mistake in front of others
- wanting to be good at something they try
- wanting to succeed
- worrying
- feeling misunderstood
- getting sick
- wanting to be important
- having opinions
- wanting to be in charge more
- wondering what their purpose is
- relationships (at different levels because of gender)

Use their preteen-world stuff to reach! When you use their world examples, you're showing preteens you really care about them. You'll touch their hearts and minds. In turn, they'll bring their friends to learn too. You'll reach heart after heart and mind after mind.

Use their preteen-world stuff to preach! NOT!! Don't preach to preteens. They get sermons from parents and schoolteachers, police officers and firefighters, even friends and neighbors. Great teaching involves the students in discussions. Teaching segments should be short and interactive. Preaching is telling them stuff for more than, say, five minutes. Save the preteen-world stuff for teaching and reaching and skip the preaching.

DO DIFFERENCES MATTER?

We all know there's a big difference between boys and girls at this age. Preteen boys are still boys—complete with short attention spans, boyish silliness, and energy that must be released often. Most relationships are based on poking, pushing, and making goofy noises. Their world, for the most part, revolves around themselves and the stuff they're interested in (and it's not girls or reading or sitting around).

Preteen girls are still girls in age, but act more like teens. They're into crafts, fashion, talking (a lot), and talking some more. Their world also revolves around themselves and the stuff they're interested in (and it's not poking or pushing or immature boy stuff). If you've been in a room with preteens for an hour, you already know this.

So what do you do about their differences? Does it really matter? Actually it does matter and there are plenty of ways to use their differences to a good advantage. In large-group times, preteens really get going when boys compete against girls. They're very competitive against each other. You can keep the score pretty even by using questions that'll appeal to what each group is most interested in. Preteens have some things in common, too, believe it or not. They all relate to being scared of things or wanting to be good at things they try. At SuperStart! events we asked preteens about being scared and everyone had something they wanted to say. Make good use of the things they have in common when teaching a large group, and use their differences to a good advantage in small groups.

It's wise to divide students into gender-specific small groups. The boys' groups need to do something active before sitting down. If you don't let the boys be active, they'll just explode pretty quickly. Don't expect boys to spill their guts or have an extended conversation about even the most exciting, relevant topic. But it's a real home run when you do get boys talking. The girls' groups need to talk some about their lives or do a craft. They'll tend to be more dramatic and talk a lot about their experiences and feelings. Make sure you still use examples from their world, though. Exercising the boys but then explaining the Greek meanings of the words in the Scripture won't work. And chatting with the girls about all the

A LEADER'S THOUGHTS

"All my guys like video games, so I use video games in my explanations. One time I got a new, popular video game. When I played the game, I was stumped about what to do for this one thing. I gave the game guide to my guys and asked them to use the guide to help me figure it out. Then I explained that the Bible works the same as a game guide; it helps us when we're stumped. They really got into that lesson."

—Patrick Snow

gory details of gouging out Samson's eyes won't work either. You get the idea.

PRETEENS CAN TELL

I don't need to look or act like a preteen to get into their world. Trust me on this—don't try. I'm not a preteen so I don't act like one. If I do, I'll just be hokey and unbelievable. Preteens can tell a wannabe a mile away. I do try to have lots of energy as I show them that I'm interested in what they like. When they talk with me, I let them know that what they're talking about is important. I try to talk about the things they're interested in and use their terminology. I refer to current movies and music. I use stories that tell about things I've learned and try put my stories in the context of things preteens can relate to. So I don't talk about paying taxes, getting married, or disciplining children. I'm not always good at playing their video games or sports, but that's OK with them. They can tell when I'm genuinely interested in them and when I'm not.

You'll know you've invaded their world by the look in their eyes. Are they looking at you? Are their eyes sparkling? Are they sitting on the edge of their seats clinging to every word? You start a sentence and they finish it. Are the students jumping up and down saying, "Pick me, pick me!" Are the students diligently trying to find something in their Bibles? Not in my experience! Honestly, sometimes you just don't know if you're getting through to preteens or not. Sometimes they're engaged and right with you. Other times they may be all over the place.

Don't freak out if they go wild on you. It happens, and they may still be listening. When you're ministering every week, they will get crazy on you at times, but they'll still hear what God wants them to hear. Sometimes you'll think a lesson was a disaster, but when the students come back next week, they say or do something that lets you know they thought about what you said. Just because they don't act engaged, doesn't mean they didn't get it.

NEW FRONTIERS

Four essential relationships for preteens

Preteens are just starting to figure out relationships. Preteens have already had relationships with friends, their parents, and maybe even Jesus, but they're just starting to realize how important those relationships are to them. They're starting to find meaning from their relationships. The relationships they have with their friends, parents, and Jesus are all changing and gaining new meaning. They're at the age where they're thinking more about their relationships with others. They're starting to think about what's going on around them and realizing they're not the only ones to have feelings and ideas. Preteens are also experiencing the transition from concrete to abstract thinking and this also affects their growing relationships.

RELATIONSHIPS WITH FRIENDS

Until now, preteens would hang out with others because they went to the same school or because they lived in the same neighborhood. Now they're starting to realize they have choices when it comes to friends. And they're learning that their choices in friends can make a difference.

Preteens are finding out how much their friendships mean to them. They're exploring relationships with their peers, and during this time, there can be lots of awkwardness. One thing preteen leaders can do is help preteens develop healthy friendships. When leaders help preteens develop healthy friendships among their Christian peers, the preteens have been given a gift that will help their faith in Jesus grow. What can be better than a great Christian friend?

With girls, it's a real roller coaster ride. For boys, it's still all about playing. For girls, it's all "She said" or "I feel." Relationships are a big deal to boys too, just not as important as they are for girls. There's usually not much of a relationship between boys and girls at this age. Girls are interested in boys, but boys are interested in just being goofy.

A great example of the differences between boys and girls at this age happened at our SuperStart! event one year. We had a track around the edge of a large room for a go-kart race. When we opened the doors, the boys came in and just started running around the track. Some of the girls ran too, but most of them stood around the edge, watching and talking about the boys. The boys didn't even know anyone was watching. They related to the other boys by running with them and were oblivious to the girls watching. It was different for the boys who were midway through their 6th grade year. These boys would never run around the track, unless they were trying to win the race and get the attention of the girls. As you work with preteens you'll see the differences in the way they act.

A NEW RELATIONSHIP

There are four essential relationships for preteens: Jesus, parents, friends, and adult leaders. Of these, the relationship that's the most established is the one with their parents. The newest relationship for preteens will be with the adult leaders in their preteen ministry. They've probably had Sunday school teachers before, but leaders of preteen small groups fill a bigger role.

Preteens are exposed to more issues than ever before through the many forms of media and possibly extensive travel. Preteens like to think they can navigate all of this new stuff on their own, but they really need help. As a small-group leader, I can help guide my boys through lots of issues, including their successes and failures. I have it easy though. I get the guys' groups, so I don't have nearly as many issues as the girls' leaders do. You know this already if you've been around preteens for a while. It's not that girls have more issues. They just talk about the issues more because they're thinking about them more. They are also more open and add more drama when they talk about their situations.

APPROPRIATE RELATIONSHIPS

I truly enjoy hanging out with preteens. I'm not their buddy or best friend, though. As an adult leader, I have to keep in mind that there is a definite line I cannot cross. When I become a preteen's best friend, that's crossing the line. As a ministry leader, I have to guide other ministry volunteers to avoid crossing that line. Safety is huge and crossing the line jeopardizes that safety. It's great for adult leaders to attend students' sports events or performances once in a while. But contacting a student outside of the class or youth group setting without his or her parent's knowledge, that's crossing the line. It's OK for adult leaders to call or send their students e-mails or text messages as long as parents know and approve, and as long as these contacts are not on a regular basis. Building relationships with preteens means building relationships with their parents. It's not just about gaining trust with the students, but also with the parents. When new students become involved, get to know their parents as well.

I like to build relationships with my preteens and that comes over time. Adult leaders can send birthday wishes and "I missed you at church" postcards or e-mails. (I'm terrible at this!) I like to think of myself as a mentoring friend to my preteens. We look forward to seeing each other once a week at church. I listen to them and pray for them. I've been to events for a couple of the guys in my group and I always sit with their parents. The boys talk about having me over to their homes and I consider that a compliment. For me, it doesn't usually happen, though. But I always follow one important rule—never meet with a preteen one-on-one. For the most part, I always meet with preteens in a group.

I want to be a model for my preteens—a model of Christ's love and grace, integrity and fun, a healthy relationship. I'm an authority figure to them, not a preteen. I want them to trust me and listen to me. There's trouble when there's no authority in a large or small group. Most preteens don't listen to or trust someone who hasn't earned their respect. My first few weeks with a new group of boys are always a huge challenge because of this. It's also why substitutes have a hard time. That's why it's so important to commit to working with a group for an extended period of time.

THE MOST IMPORTANT RELATIONSHIP

While some students have made commitments to Jesus, many others haven't. It's their relationships with Jesus that I most want to cultivate in my students. It's the whole reason I do what I do. Even students who have made commitments to Jesus are just beginning to learn the more abstract aspects of a relationship with Him. They're somewhere between Jesus being like a Santa and Jesus being their real best friend. I get to help students begin this new sort of experience, one that hopefully will continue to grow throughout their lives. It's pretty humbling when you think about it. I can help students understand that knowing Jesus is more than just something their parents want them to do.

So I start finding ways for students to own their faith. I let them pray their own prayers. I ask them to tell what a Scripture means. I ask them to help serve. Preteens are really good at serving. Getting them involved in these spiritual disciplines helps them understand more about their relationships with Jesus. I want students to know they have the choice about whether to come to church and whether to make a commitment to Jesus or not. If they make the choice to commit to Jesus, then I've helped make an eternal impact on their lives.

MAKING IT STICK

What makes great lessons

When it comes to teaching and leading preteens, there's no one right way to do it. I think it's best to have the biggest possible "bag of ideas" and then to pull different things out of it as they're needed. I have in my bag all the info I've already learned about preteens. My bag also has some other pretty cool things in it, such as knowing which popular song or video clip to use. Whenever I see something that preteens are talking about or involved in, I add that to my bag. I watch commercials on TV (did I say that, really?), check out preteen books and magazines, and listen to parents. Parents usually know what their preteens are into and thinking about. I never know where I'll find something new for my bag.

Learning happens when lessons stick. Great lessons are made up of several things: fun, a teaching time, a small-group time, and worship. Getting the right balance of these elements and using preteen-world examples and ideas make lessons come alive and stick. I wish I could say I always get it right, but I don't. Preteens are forgiving, though. That's just one of the reasons I love working with them.

IT HAS TO BE FUN

The first thing about teaching is that fun has to be a part of it. I don't know the reason behind it, I just know it's true. Students love to have fun. Preteens are still in the play mode, especially the boys. They love being crazy, playing games, and making each other laugh. They'll join in physical challenges (Who can stand on one foot the longest?) and participate in unusual challenges (What's the wildest thing you can do with your tongue?). It may not seem as though fun should be a part of great lessons, but it is. During fun times I try to model good relationships and help students build good ones too. I'm also helping them get ready to pay attention to the serious part of the lesson.

UNSTRUCTURED PLAY

There are two kinds of play—structured and unstructured. Both are great; I just use them at different times. Unstructured play is when students are free to choose what they want to do. To do this, there has to be room for students to have some free reign but still be safe. It takes a little ingenuity to make a space for the boys (some girls too) to be wild and goofy, as well as have a place for the girls (and some boys) to sit and talk. Now don't get me wrong; this isn't a time when students are out of control—not at all. I want the students to have a good time and go a little crazy if they want, but at the same time, I don't let them just run around and get really wild. I don't think anyone has fun when that's happening.

At SuperStart! events, unstructured play is where we set up lots of big games for preteens to get involved in. We put the games in hallways or large rooms before each session begins. I've seen other successful preteen ministries set up lots of fun stuff like foosball, video games, carpetball, and couches right in the room where they will be meeting. Preteens who come early can hang out and have fun. I don't tell students they must do this or that. I just encourage them to do things with their friends or the adult leaders. The goal is for the time to be relational and fun. Unstructured time is important because it builds excitement and allows students to get out their energy so you can rein them in when it is time for the lesson.

STRUCTURED PLAY

Structured play is when I have the students all participate in a specific energetic or goofy game. Competition is important in the preteen world. It's a part of every structured game. The boys' idea of fun competition is anything loud and crazy with lots of laughter. Girls are more relational, so in a game of dodge ball, winning isn't that important. They don't mind having to sit on the sidelines because they can talk with their friends. If you've worked with preteens, you know it's completely different with the boys. With boys, it's all about winning. If they're losing, it's the end of the world—at least until the next game. As long as we're talking about competition, we'd better bring up the subject of fairness. This is important! You'd better know the rules inside and out and be a good referee. If there is a sketchy call or if someone is trying to get away with cheating, well, that'll be more important than who's winning or losing.

One great thing about preteens is that they'll submit to rules, even if you make them up in the middle of a game. The preteen pastor at the church where I've volunteered does this all the time. He'll make up this crazy, fun game and midway through the game he will realize that the students are getting a little too crazy. So he'll throw out a new rule. I'm amazed! The students go along with whatever the new rule is. They're funny like that.

TEACHING TIME

There should even be an element of play in the teaching time. I pretty much always start with fun stuff, whether I'm doing a large-group session like a SuperStart! event or a small-group session with my boys at church. That's where I start. Then when it comes to the lesson, I get serious. You can't be silly when you're making the main point or students won't take it seriously. I make sure I am excited about the lesson, but not like it's a joke. To me, it's OK to tell the students things like "Shhh," "I need you guys to listen to this," "Hear me say this," "This is the coolest thing," or "We're going to be serious now." When I'm talking with them, I want them to really listen and be excited. I often say things like "Check this out!" or "This is amazing!" I've found I need to say these things in both large and small groups. Yes, I want the students to have fun, but I also want them to take the lesson seriously. Preteens aren't always able to pick up on the cues of when to settle down, so I just tell them. But I don't get upset with them. They're pretty respectful if I give them the heads-up that it's time to get quiet, especially if I've given them time to get their energy out.

To make a lesson stick with preteens, I do everything I can to make it interactive, apply it to where they're at, and help them understand what it means to them. At SuperStart! events, students watch a story unfold and learn how to figure things out by watching the characters on stage. Preteens are big observers. I also like to guide them to figure out the solution. Guiding them through the process to make their own connection is more powerful than telling them. They'll remember the lesson much longer.

CHECK THIS OUT:
YESTERDAY VS. TODAY

When choosing preteen lesson topics, consider these facts:

Yesterday's preteens faced
- an age of individual reason
- physical and mental changes
- confronting personal morality and values
- sexuality and marriage

Today's preteens face the same issues, but also face
- the fragmentation of the family
- knowledge and exposure to sexuality
- technological advances
- knowledge and exposure to violence
- neutral moral and religious values

Comparison by Tony Jones, National Coordinator of Emergent Village. Used by permission.

Another way to make the lesson stick is to repeat the main point as often as possible. At SuperStart! events, we try to put the main point in a catchy phrase of some kind, such as, "If you're wise, you'll shine." And there's more than one way to repeat the point. Students can say it, write it, read it from a big screen, say it with leaders, turn and say it to partners, or the boys can try to out-yell the girls. I'm sure you can think of more ways too. The more ways you can involve the students, the more likely they are to remember what you've talked about.

CHANGE IT UP

There is a limit to how long preteens will pay attention, especially if they're sitting still and just listening. Someone told me that he expects students to pay attention one minute for every year of age the students are. So if the students are 10 years old, that means they'll sit still and listen for 10 minutes. Maturity of the students will make a difference in this time, but probably only by a plus or minus of five minutes. Now this doesn't mean you should only teach for 10 minutes and let the students play for 50 minutes. Not at all. It means that about every 10 minutes you need to change up what's happening. You can show a video clip, lead in singing some worship songs, have students turn and do something with partners, or have some students come up front and talk with you. There are lots of things you can do and it's still teaching. It's just that you won't spend more than ten minutes at one time talking to the students.

Another fact to remember is that preteens must release energy. To me, energy release is a critical component of a lesson. Preteens' bodies are changing and their energy gets all balled up inside of them. You have to give them opportunities to let this energy out because it's as though you're battling two forces—attention span and energy. Energy release is exactly what it sounds like: letting students release some of their energy. Some leaders have students stand and jump up and down. I like to make it a little more subtle so they don't know that's what I'm doing. Either way works. Energy release is any time you get preteens moving. When you're planning, just make sure you'll get them moving every ten minutes or so.

What about using object lessons with preteens? I'd say object lessons are a must for preteens. The best object lessons seem to be those that are interactive. I'd rather not teach without something interactive. There was a time when about once a month I'd take a goofy little red suitcase to class. Every time there was something different in it. It was a big mystery and the students always wanted to guess what was inside. The object always had something to do with the lesson and it was up to the students to try to figure out what it was.

If I'm going to have just one object up front, then I try to make sure it's either mysterious or involves at least one student, if not several of them. One year at the SuperStart! events we used robes and slime. We had students come to the front and wear robes. While we were giving the gospel message, we used slime to represent sin and poured the slime on the kids wearing the robes. That worked pretty well.

THE RIGHT BALANCE

A healthy balance between being goofy and talking with preteens on their level about serious topics is important. Preteens need to have fun. They also need to understand that there's a time to be serious. There's an important reason why these students are in your room. They're in your room so that you can help them connect to Christ. That is a serious matter. Taking your teaching seriously shows that you care about your preteens. If you're never serious, your students

A LEADER'S THOUGHTS

"Your ministry is an extension of you, so what you're passionate about is what you'll infuse into your ministry."

—Craig Wilson,
Children's Pastor, California

won't take anything you say seriously. I use silly and goofy stuff during the icebreaker and attention-getting times. Then when I teach, I get serious. That's when we focus on the "this is what you're going through and this is how God can help you" stuff.

This silly vs. serious idea is a cool model of most preteens—they're a lot silly, but also able to get fairly serious. They can get serious sometimes even without you having to tell them. That's one thing that makes preteens different from children. They do take a lot of things seriously in their lives.

LARGE AND SMALL GROUPS

There's a difference between what you can do in a large group of preteens and what you can do in a small group. Large group time is for the fun, structured games. It's also the time for giving students the big picture, talking with them about what the Scripture means, and helping them think about how the lesson can relate to their lives. I like to think that during the large-group time I'm laying down the dots in a big dot-to-dot picture. These dots include the Bible passage, relating Bible truths to what the students are experiencing in their lives right now, and an illustration or two that preteens can relate to. But all of this has to be short and sweet. If the teaching time goes for more than 15 minutes, I need to offer an energy release of some sort.

Students love to share their stories. I let them do this in both large and small groups. If I ask for volunteers to share in a large group, like at SuperStart! events, I do my best to make sure they're students who will be willing to talk once they get up front. I tell them, "I need someone who's willing to come up here and talk a lot about ___." When I have preteens come up front and share stories, I make sure everyone listens to them.

I've found that I have to be prepared for anything. I get lots of surprises when I have students share. No matter what the students say, I consider it awesome that they were willing to talk and I thank them for sharing—even if it didn't work. It's great to have students share their stories because they learn a lot from listening to their peers.

CONNECTING THE DOTS

But to help students go deep, I need to talk with them in a small group. Deep thinking requires guidance at this age. It's in the small groups where the dots are really connected. Connecting the dots is a big deal, and it's best if preteens do this on their own. If I have to connect the dots for them, I haven't done a good job of getting into their world and helping them think through the major points. Guiding preteens to connect the dots is a lot of work, but it's really worth the effort.

Students can go deep, so I set high expectations for them. They usually know more than I think they do. I need to challenge them, push them to think, and show them how the lesson relates to them personally. Students can then look at the Scripture as more than just some words on a page that they have to read. I have to start with something they're familiar with and then ask them to relate it to something they may not be as familiar with. One time I was talking with the boys in my small group about discouraging versus encouraging words. I asked each of them to tell about a name he had been called. They all had one and they didn't like it. After that, they were much more understanding of the Scripture about how the words we use affect others.

TECHNOLOGY

Technology is another big topic that comes up whenever I talking about teaching. I always recommend using students instead of technology. Here's what I mean. If you can use a student to explain a concept, then don't use a video clip of someone explaining the concept. Preteens really do learn a lot from each other. And it's always better to have preteens do something rather than watch someone else do it. That being said, there are some exceptions. Sometimes there's a great video clip that illustrates a point in a way you just couldn't do in class. Or maybe a video clip can illustrate something or make a point more quickly. Preteens love video, so I do use video to mix things up, get the kids' attention, or introduce an idea or problem. It's also fun to use a slide show of my preteens when they were at an event or doing some activity.

Preteens are far more familiar with technology than I am because they've grown up with it. They all know how to make the DVD player work when I get stumped. And they all know how to play video games—and it's not just a boy thing. At SuperStart! events one year we used a corn maze video game to make a point, and the students were totally involved. We had this maze on the big screen and the students had to decide whether to go right or left to avoid this crazy farmer character. The preteens were competing against one of the SuperStart! cast members on stage and it was very obvious I was helping her win. They got pretty upset with me for a while! But I used the experience to make a point about where to get help. A rule I try to follow is that I don't use technology to make the main point. And I never use it to fill time. If I finish early, it's better to give students free time than to turn on a video.

MAKE IT YOUR OWN

One last thing about teaching. When you use curriculum, make it your own. I never read right from the teacher guide when I'm with students. I read the teacher guide ahead of time and make notes, usually on sticky notes, and put those in my Bible marking the Scripture passage for the day. I show students I care when I come to class prepared. I also look for ways to tailor the lesson to make it fit my group of students. I go through the curriculum and think, *I have something else I'd rather do here,* or *My students would understand this better if I used another example.* I never feel like I have to use a lesson just as it's laid out. I don't think curriculum publishers expect that either. They want to give you plenty of ideas so you can adapt the curriculum as needed. They also understand how unique your preteens and your situation can be. Trust me, curriculum publishers won't be offended if you take their ideas and change them up a bit to reach your students.

GREAT EXPECTATIONS

What preteens can do

There are a lot of things preteens can do. They constantly amaze me with what they can do—and I hear this over and over from other preteen leaders too. For example, preteens are really good at sharing their faith. They're not self-conscious like middle school or high school students. They don't usually feel silly telling their friends about Jesus. They don't think there's anything wrong with inviting their friends to church either. They're great evangelists. About halfway through sixth grade, though, some of them get self-conscious and don't share their faith much any more. As a preteen leader, you can help your students by focusing in on their abilities and talents and encouraging them to grow in those areas.

A *TD Monthly™* report indicates that preteen spending has now been pegged in the billions of dollars. Reyne Rice of NPD Funworld research credits preteens for "bringing $3 billion of new money to the marketplace." And author and consultant Anne Sutherland believes preteens are more than simple cash cows. They are "sophisticated, savvy, and influential."

While preteens often want new gadgets, Sutherland argues it goes beyond that. "Our research shows that over 60 percent of Tween boys make their own choices for fast food and over 70 percent of boys and girls at age 13 make their own clothing choices. . . . General Motors believes that boys under 10 know what cars they want to drive when they graduate to driving status."

www.toydirectory.com/monthly/june2003/
Tweens_Generations.asp

THEY CAN TEACH AND LEAD

Preteens can teach. Now that's not to say that all of them can teach, but in every group, I always find at least a few students who are fairly good at teaching. I need to coach them and help them, but they're great about telling others what they're figuring out about their faith or what the Bible says.

There's always one boy in my group who is a natural leader. The other boys all look up to him and want to hang out with him. The funny thing is that this boy usually doesn't even notice this is happening. At the preteen age, most preteens are not too aware of their leadership abilities.

Preteens can help with worship. The girls may be more willing than the boys to be up front singing. But there's more to worship than just singing. There are students who can play instruments and students who can help with the sound or DVD player. There are other students who can read Scripture or help serve Communion. Craig Wilson is a great preteen leader who encourages his students to lead worship. He has a monthly worship service that's completely led by students. Now that's cool—and that's leadership.

THEY CAN SERVE

Service is huge for preteens. They're really good at it. They thrive on serving. I know of preteen ministries where students serve at retirement homes, parks, other churches, their own church, and homeless shelters. Preteens can help raise money for mission trips for the older students by washing cars, making and selling pizzas, and even just asking people. Preteens can help prepare lessons and then help teach them to younger students on special occasions. They can serve as small-group leaders during combined services with younger children. They can make things for kids in schools and shelters. They can look for lonely people in their neighborhood and visit them (with parents' permission, of course) or take them things they've made. The more opportunities you give preteens to serve, the better.

Louie, a preteen minister I know, has a team of student leaders called the pit crew. One thing the pit crew does is put out the 80 beanbag chairs the preteens use and then they pray over the chairs, asking God to move during the service. Some of the pit crew students help with running lights, sound, and PowerPoint during the service. Others are greeters and take new students and their parents on tours of the facility. It's cool how these students are learning to use their gifts and talents to serve.

Craig's students started cleaning up a schoolyard on Sunday afternoons. The principal of the school was ecstatic because it saved the school a lot of money by not having to hire custodians to do the job. And the students were proud because they were doing something that matters. The preteens were also bridge-building with the community—and that is cool!

These preteen leaders spend a lot of time working and serving right alongside their students because preteens aren't usually ready to serve on their own. In fact, this brings up an important point. Preteens are just getting started in serving. They need help and guidance in knowing how to serve. They may also need training in how to do some things. And it's great for students to have adults serving alongside them.

THEY CAN PRAY AND BE CREATIVE

Preteens are good at praying. They can pray together in their small groups, pray with partners, or pray by themselves. Some students are even confident enough to pray in front of a large group. If students pray in a large group, I like to know them well enough that I have confidence that they'll actually pray. At SuperStart! events, I find that some students volunteer to pray just because they want to be picked and get attention, but when I ask them to pray, they're suddenly speechless.

Preteens are really great at acting things out. They're very creative and have active imaginations. Sometimes they're kind of silly, but they always have creative ideas. As with everything else, if I tell them the expectations, they'll usually rise to them.

The key to success in getting preteens to fulfill expectations is to train them and give them support. Students at this age are still learning lots of things, so I have to tell them the expectations and coach them well. I never expect students to take the place of leaders, but they can assist leaders. Once you get preteens started, they are a valuable asset and can show amazing initiative.

Just like adults, preteens do best at the things God wired them to do. Serving is the one thing they're all interested in because it's something they all can do. I like to think that serving is one place where students can find their gifts. Those preteens who want to lead worship now will probably be the worship leaders in junior high, high school, and beyond. Those students who the others just naturally follow are probably those who have gifts of leadership. Those who want to help teach now are probably those with the gifts of teaching. Now is a perfect time to help students explore their God-given gifts and help them begin learning how to use those gifts.

COOPERATION?
IT CAN HAPPEN!

The balance of structure and fun

Preteens are great to work with because they'll still do what I ask of them. In a high-energy situation like we have at SuperStart! events, students really need to know who's in charge. I have to take an authoritative position with rules and stuff like that. If I set the proper expectations, then students will usually meet them. The key is to make sure the students know what I want from them.

PREPARATION IS IMPORTANT

Leaders and teachers who really understand preteens usually don't have huge classroom management issues. Good teachers don't focus on the teaching, but rather on the learning. One thing you can do that really helps with classroom management is to be prepared. My friend Louie, a great preteen leader, taught me this. He never reads directly from a curriculum guide. He uses one, for sure, but he uses it way before class begins. By the time class starts, he knows the material and he's tailored it to fit his students. In fact, if you ask most successful preteen leaders, they'll tell you that they always do a ton of preparation before each session. They don't just read through the curriculum, but they make notes and decide what to use and not use. They customize the curriculum for their students. Some large-group leaders memorize what they're going to say, Scripture and all. But they don't just repeat their memorized lines; they add examples that relate to their students and insert things they've thought about while preparing.

INVOLVEMENT AND EXPECTATIONS ARE IMPORTANT

Another thing you can do that really helps with classroom management is to involve the students. Leaders and teachers who understand preteens know preteens need to be involved in what they are learning. I usually have the students read Scripture and answer questions about it, because preteens usually listen to their peers. Students can also be a part of the Bible story, talk with a partner, or participate in an activity that illustrates the lesson.

Expectations are important too. If I don't let students know what I want, there's not much chance they'll be able to meet my expectations. So I'm clear about setting expectations. For example, I'll tell students I need them to listen for five minutes and then they will talk with each other or do some fun activity.

Preteens still need to have structure even though they've moved up from children's ministry. They like surprises, but for the most part, they need to know what to expect. I think they like some routine and structure, as most of us do. Preteens want to know what they're going to do first, what they're going to do next, and what they're going to do after that. Even if we follow the same basic structure every week, I always keep things moving and make sure the students are involved so they're not bored. I can count on this: if they do get bored, they'll let me know.

When I'm in charge of a small group, the students in my group know I'm in charge too. I'm not a big disciplinarian, but the students do know the expectations. I expect students to respect each other and listen to what others have to say. When dealing with students who are just having a rough day, it's best to give them options. I've seen really effective small-group leaders give a student two choices, such as "You can sit here next to me while I read or you can read it to me." That way, the leader has told the student what is expected and also allowed the student to have some say in how to meet that expectation. It's important for students to be held accountable for their choices and know there will be consequences for wrong choices. If there is no follow-through, the students definitely won't take expectations and limits seriously.

RULES ARE IMPORTANT

The most successful preteen ministries I've seen have simple, easy-to-follow rules. Those preteen leaders and teachers do a great job of communicating the rules. Often students learn the rules without the teacher or leader even saying, "Here's my list of rules you need to follow."

My preteen minister friend Joe told me about the rules he has for the students in his preteen ministry. Joe gives a copy of the rules to parents at a parent meeting and he gives a copy to all the preteen volunteers during training. His rules follow the letters *GOD*—*G*ive others your undivided attention; *O*bey the rules; and *D*on't invade others' space. These are the same rules as for the elementary program, so the preteen students already know them. The difference is that the rules aren't reviewed every week. Joe goes over them once in the fall and then he or other teachers remind students occasionally when an issue comes up.

Katie, another successful preteen leader, has only three rules too. They are: Respect God and others, Only bring your Bible, and Don't touch anything more complicated than a folding chair. They're simple and easy to remember. They also set important boundaries for the students.

ENERGY RELEASE IS IMPORTANT

Another thing you can do that really helps with classroom management is to plan for times of energy release. Energy release is critically important. Every 10 to 15 minutes, you need to let students release their energy by letting them get up and move around. Like I've said before, the boys especially will just explode if you don't give them ways to let out their energy. I intentionally plan ways to get everyone up and moving, even if it's just for a minute or two. At SuperStart! events we use high-energy worship, let preteens move around and get into small groups, or do some goofy, fun activity to find out who will be picked to come on stage. These all work to get students up and moving for a minute.

THE RIGHT RATIO IS IMPORTANT

Another thing you can do that really helps with classroom management is have the right ratio of leaders to students. When I'm in front of a large group, I can't be the disciplinarian for individual students. I can help the whole group calm down or become involved in an activity, but I can't (and shouldn't) address individual students. That's one of the reasons we have a five-to-one ratio for our SuperStart! events. We tell preteen leaders that they really need to bring one adult for every five preteens who attend. Without this adult presence in the large group, students have a much harder time paying attention and knowing what's expected of them. Things go really well when we have the adults with their students, interacting with them and with us. It'll work the same for your large-group time too.

The adults sitting with the students are the ones who can help students know what's appropriate behavior. An adult working one-on-one with students is far better for the students. It saves them embarrassment and doesn't give undue attention to those students who are only looking for some attention. I learned this from Katie. Her volunteers know they are there to serve and work with the preteens. They sit *with* their students, not in the back. It's so cool to watch her boys worship because the adult guy who's sitting with them is worshiping right along with them. As Craig, a great preteen leader, would remind me, trying to solve an issue from the front isn't relational either, and preteens are so relational. Allowing a student to solve a problem with his or her adult leader is far more relational, and therefore far more effective. I'm sure you can apply this to your ministry with preteens.

During small-group time, a good ratio is one adult leader for every six to eight preteens. I usually have five or six boys in my small group. I don't think I'd want more than about eight in my small group. I wouldn't be able to involve each of the boys as well. When I have fewer than five boys, it's not as much fun and we don't seem to discuss as much. If you're starting with a very small number of students, you can still have fun and engage them in interesting discussions. As the number of students increases, you'll find the fun factor increases too.

It's really important to strike the right balance between structure and fun. I try to keep in mind that preteens are usually just trying to have a good time and that they sometimes forget how their energy and their actions affect others.

WILL BOYS SING?

Guiding preteens in worship

O f course boys will sing, but it's not always easy to get them to do so. At SuperStart! events, we work to make sure that most of the music is energetic and upbeat. It's OK to do some quieter songs, but not all the time.

I'm not a worship leader. You'll never see me up front when we're doing worship at SuperStart! events. If I were to lead worship it would not be pretty or effective. So everything I know I've learned from watching others. We've had great worship leaders for SuperStart! events and I've heard about some fantastic preteen worship at a number of churches. The following are some things they all seem to have in common.

MUSIC

The most effective worship leaders are ones who take the time to teach preteens what they're singing about. That's a key for getting the students to sing. If we help them understand what the words mean, they'll be more likely to sing. Other times, they just need some help understanding why we sing to God. There are lots of ways worship leaders can help students understand the importance of singing to worship God. Worship leaders can also help students see the significance of worship in their own lives. Effective worship leaders briefly explain a few of these things before a song or as worship begins. Again, students learn without ever realizing they're being taught.

The preteen worship leaders I talk with constantly tell me how hard it is to find age-appropriate music. Preteens have outgrown the repetitious choruses of children's church, and much of the junior high and high school music is too advanced for them. They still have a limited range they can sing in too; they can't sing too high or too low, especially the boys. There just aren't too many people who get what preteens want in Christian music. So when you find some music that works for your preteens, latch onto it. Preteens don't mind the repetition of their favorite songs, so don't worry about using them frequently.

At SuperStart! events, we've gone back and forth about whether to use hand motions and movement while preteens sing. Hand motions can be sign language that's done for some of the words in songs. These

A LEADER'S THOUGHTS

"We try to create an environment that is conducive to teaching. Rather than just singing songs each week, we often pause to talk about what we're singing and reflect about the significance it has in our lives."

—Louie Murillo,
Family Life Minister, Texas

can be cool, but it seems to be more of an elementary thing to do rather than a preteen thing. Movement that appeals to preteens is more like jumping, spinning, and waving hands and arms in the air. The first year we did SuperStart! we didn't use much movement with songs and we got lots of feedback asking for more. So now we include lots of movement but not much in the way of hand motions. I'm not sure movement is always necessary, but it is good to get the students up and moving. Getting them moving does seem to keep them more interested in the singing.

I've noticed that the person who's leading the singing can influence who sings along. It doesn't matter who leads the singing, but he or she has to be dynamic and able to appeal to the boys as well as to the girls. If you have a woman lead the singing, maybe having a guy helping up front would be good, and vice versa. If you have a guy leading, it sure helps the boys join in. I think the most important thing, though, is that the leader understands preteens, their music, and their singing ability.

At SuperStart! events we always use a band. Having live musicians is a huge component of our weekend. Maybe using live music gives the event more of a concert feel. It might not always be possible to use a band. CDs and DVDs are fine too, but they have to be really good and completely appropriate. Otherwise, I've found they're a big turnoff to the students.

The first year at SuperStart! events, we used a wheel that had a picture of a boy, a girl, an adult, and one of all three. We had different students spin the wheel and wherever it stopped, that's who had to dance. This was not during worship, however. It did get the boys and the adults actively involved, so when it came to worship, they participated. We've also tried having the girls sing one part and the guys sing another part. We've had competitions with the boys trying to out-sing the girls. When we do these things, though, we do our best to make sure that the main focus is worship of God, not competition with each other. This is really important to me. The focus always has to be worshiping God, not something else.

NOT JUST MUSIC

I know that worship is not just about the music. Worship is telling God you love Him and praising Him. In fact, worship should be everything we do. It's good to start teaching students about this too. Don't get me wrong. Many students probably have been worshiping God before they became preteens, but at this age, they're better able to connect the dots. Their worship can take on a much deeper meaning as they begin to think more abstractly.

Preteens can and should be involved during a worship service. Many of them can pray, collect the offering, serve communion, and read Scripture. Many of them have great testimonies and are willing to share them too. Involving as many students as possible in these areas of worship is great. Preteens may not have a full understanding of all they are doing, but they can keep learning as they continue to worship each week. They may not have a complete grasp of everything, but they can get a start on it. Growing in worship is a lifelong journey. We're just helping the students get on the road.

Because worship is not just singing, it's good to offer other opportunities within the worship time. I know worship leaders who have preteens write, speak, draw, paint, and even sculpt their praise to God. Instead of singing, students can stomp, rap, or drum their praises too. No one can do all of these every week, but it's fun to insert something different in the worship on occasion. There's something very cool that happens when students use different types of expressions in their worship.

TRANSITIONS AND LEADERS

Transitions are pretty important too. Preteens don't just switch gears instantly. I don't either, come to think of it. At SuperStart!

events, we have certain times when the students know we're going to worship partly by the transitions we use. I know artful worship leaders who use music as transitions. They start worship by having preteens sing great, upbeat music, and then later help students transition into a more reflective mood by the choice

A LEADER'S THOUGHTS

"It's amazing to watch our sixth grade boys change during worship when our male leaders are right there participating. They go from arms crossed to clapping and jumping."

—**Katie Gerber,** *Preteen Ministry Associate*, Indiana

of music. These worship leaders coach and guide the students in worship without making it overly obvious. I love these worship leaders because they've worked hard to guide preteens in worship and worship becomes an expression of who the preteens are and how much they love the Lord.

What helps preteens stay focused on worship as much as anything is having small-group leaders sit with their students and genuinely join them in worship. If all of the small-group leaders and other adults are sitting in the back and chatting, the students won't see any importance in what they're doing, no matter what is said or done up front. It's so cool to see adults and students worshiping together.

It's great to have a part in teaching preteens about worship and leading them in it. We're hopeful that some of what we do during SuperStart! events and the things you do week in and week out will encourage students to live their lives in worshipful ways.

YOUR BEST FRIENDS

The crucial role of parents

Believe it or not, when it comes to leading preteens, parents are our best friends. Have you noticed how often parents come up in our conversations and how often they've come up in this book? Parents are an important part of every aspect of a preteen ministry. They provide information and support and fill a number of other important roles.

All of the successful preteen leaders I've talked with tell me that parents are their greatest asset. When these preteen leaders talk about parents, they use words and phrases such as *awesome, great, incredible, can't live without them,* and *the reason our preteen ministry works.*

PARENTS AS INFORMATION

Parents are an amazing source of information. If you want to know what preteens are into and what they're thinking about, ask some parents of preteens. You could talk to parents of preteens in your ministry or other parents of preteens. I know and talk with several parents whose preteens aren't in my ministry.

A LEADER'S THOUGHTS

"We are not the main spiritual influence on the students. Parents are. We have to support parents. We can't contradict them or tell students their parents are wrong. Our goal should be that we no longer have a job because the parents are so involved in their child's growth. It'll never happen, so it needs to be a strategic partnership."

—Joe Puentes,
Preteen Minister, Missouri

Parents are with their preteens seven days a week. They know what's on their preteens' minds, what they worry about, what issues are important to them, and what they're struggling with. I often talk with parents about their students and I always learn a lot. I also talk with them when I need an illustration or suggestion for a talk I'm giving. They really know what they're talking about when it comes to preteens.

CHECK THIS OUT:
PRETEENS GIVE FAMILIES MIXED MARKS

According to a nationwide survey among children ages 8 to 12, conducted by The Barna Group:

- eight of every ten adolescents (79%) feel safe when they are at home

- two out of every three (69%) say their family eats dinner together at least five nights a week

- 64% of preteens feel they can trust their parents to do what is right for the child

- a slim majority (57%) say they look forward to spending free time with their families

- one out of every three preteens (35%) say they find it easy to talk to their parents about everything that is happening in their lives

www.barna.org/FlexPage.aspx?Page=Barna Update&BarnaUpdateID=246

PARENTS AS VOLUNTEERS

Parents are key volunteers. They can do a lot of things for the preteen ministry and are usually willing to help out wherever they can. Parents will drive their cars or vans anywhere you need and take students with them. Since renting cars and vans is expensive and you still need drivers, you might as well ask parents to drive their vehicles. And, if parents are driving, they might as well chaperone when they get there. They've got an automatic small group with the students in their car or van. Upon arriving at the destination, if some vehicles only have a few students, have parents add a few extra preteens to their groups from those who were riding in the church van.

Speaking of driving cars, there are some parents who love to shop. Recruit these parents to pick up supplies you need, help you think through snacks you'll want, and even decorate your preteen area. These parents will save you tons of time and often enjoy finding the best deals on stuff, which will also save you money.

At church, parents can check students in and out, take care of administrative duties, lead small groups, and even teach the large group. The key to using parents at church is to give them clear expectations and training. Telling them what needs to be done, when it needs to be done, and how it needs to be done is helpful to them. Don't assume they know what it means to be a small-group leader or how to check in students. It's important to offer training. Give parents plenty of information, both written and verbal. Pair them up with a veteran who does things well. Encourage parents too. Parents are willing assistants if they know what to do. They can be a tremendous asset to your preteen ministry.

A LEADER'S THOUGHTS

"Parents are wonderful. Use them! They're great to have on special events and overnighters. They help you with all your small projects: copies, getting supplies, and running to Sam's Club for last minute snacks."

—Katie Gerber,
Preteen Ministry Associate,
Indiana

PARENTS AS PARTNERS

If you want preteen students, you need to partner with their parents. Without the parents, you won't have the students. It's a pretty simple formula: no parents equals no students. The parents are the ones who bring the students, pay for anything their students need, and remember the dates of all your events. Well, they remember the dates most of the time.

Parents are great promoters. If the preteen ministry is going great, parents will be out telling the pastor, their friends, and the parents of other students. They'll partner with you by bringing nieces and nephews, neighborhood preteens, students from the soccer team, and students from school. If you've helped them understand their preteens, they'll tell other parents who will bring their preteens too.

Parents are also great prayer partners. They're concerned about their preteens so they're on track to pray for them. They'll pray for you too, if you ask them. Get parents praying together—now that's a great team.

Parents can be your cheerleaders. If you're helping them with their preteens and doing your best, they'll keep cheering you on. Ministry is tough work and we all need people who encourage us and tell us what we're doing right. I've found parents can be pretty good at this. Of course, there will be some who aren't cheerleaders, but a lot of them are. Choose to listen to your cheerleaders. Let them know how valuable it is to hear from them. They'll be there for you.

This is not to say that we shouldn't listen to those parents who disagree with us. We realize there will always be those who think differently than us, and that's OK. We also realize we will mess up on occasion. We do our best not to, but we still do. Some parents are good at catching us at these times. They hold us accountable and make sure our humility is intact. That's a valuable aspect of partnering with parents.

Parents are definitely partners when it comes to funding the preteen ministry, if you think about it. Their gifts might mean

> ## A LEADER'S THOUGHTS
>
> "Parents play a vital role in our ministry. We encourage parents to be involved in their preteens' ministry. We utilize them as small-group leaders, teachers, check-in leaders, and general volunteers."
>
> **—Louie Murillo,**
> *Family Life Minister*, Texas

cool stuff for your ministry, money for trips and transportation, and even money for weekly supplies. When you look at parents, you should never just see dollar signs, but you should see their incredible value.

YOU CAN HELP

I've talked a lot about what parents can do for us. We need to remember that there's plenty we can do for parents too. When you've worked with preteens for even a little while, you begin to understand them. You can pass this understanding on to their parents. Sometimes parents think they're the only ones having certain problems with their preteens. When you assure them that they're not and help them to see options for dealing with problems, you're a star in their eyes.

Sometimes parents face big issues of their own. When you help their preteens understand a little of what's going on and are a support to the students for a time, you'll help the parents immeasurably. When you help a parent and a preteen find a way to communicate, you've made both of their lives better.

CHECK THIS OUT:
SOME PRETEEN PARENTS OUT OF TOUCH

According to one study, parents don't know much about their children's use of the Internet. The statistics show:

- 33% of preteens and teens say their parents know little or nothing about what they do online

- 22% say their parents have never discussed Internet safety with them

- 51% of parents don't know if they have software on their computers that lets them monitor where their children go online

- 42% of parents don't monitor what their children read or type in chat rooms

- 95% of parents don't understand the short-hand lingo kids use in chat rooms

www.symantec.com/norton/library/familyresource/article.jsp?aid=pr_internetsafety_and_your_tween

When you help parents better understand their preteens, you've benefited both parents and students. When you help preteens find Christ and their identities in Him rather than in the world, you've helped change their lives life for eternity. Parents will be eternally grateful for this.

YOU CAN COMMUNICATE AND TRAIN

There are lots of ways to communicate with parents. Some preteen leaders create parent newsletters, either sending them home with students or sending them via e-mail or regular mail. Some preteen leaders offer training for parents by bringing in guest speakers or by speaking themselves on a variety of topics. Of course, you can refer parents to lots of great books and Web sites as well.

You don't have to be the final authority on all things preteen. There's plenty of help for you. Share what you find with parents and they will be very grateful. Encourage parents all you can. Being a preteen leader is tough. Being the parent of a preteen is even tougher. Build up parents and let them know they're doing a good job. If you do, you'll be best friends with them.

In the greater scheme of things, you're impacting more than just the parents. You are influencing their preteens, the friends of their preteens, and even extended families. You are even influencing how your students will relate to their own children one day—so you are impacting future generations for God's kingdom too. Did you have any idea you were doing so much? I thought not.

A LEADER'S THOUGHTS

"I wish I would have learned early on to involve parents a lot more. Now I always kick off the new year with a parent meeting, give them statistics, and prepare the parents for what's coming. It opens the door for them to come to me when they're having problems."

—Craig Wilson,
Children's Pastor, California

IN AND OUT

Helping students transition in and out of preteen ministry

Preteens don't stay preteens for very long. Most preteen ministries I know only have their students for two years. That's not very long. Every year I have half of the students just entering the ministry and half of the students getting ready to leave the ministry. Making the most of those two short years requires planning.

I have learned most of the stuff about transitioning students in and out of preteen ministry from watching a number of very successful preteen ministries. I've learned that it is vital to plan ahead, communicate with other leaders, and be intentional about everything you do.

PLAN AHEAD

If you get students into your ministry well, you'll have more time to minister to them. This means planning ahead. Start in the spring to begin incorporating incoming students. Giving students the summer to get used to the preteen ministry is helpful; when fall gets going, you're in full swing.

CHECK THIS OUT:
THE IMPORTANCE OF AGE 12

Studies show that age 12 is a key transition time for kids. At that point, young people are most vulnerable to

- losing trust in parents
- losing interest in family activities
- leaning more toward popularity than morality
- questioning their future

www.barna.org/FlexPage.aspx?Page=Barna
Update&BarnaUpdateID=246

Getting the oldest students ready to move on also helps you be more effective. If you've done your job well, your oldest students will be ready and eager to move on. If you have fifth and sixth graders, this is especially true. The sixth graders begin checking out in the spring, so it's best to begin their transition then. This helps them stay engaged. Building positive anticipation for what comes next is a valuable help to students.

COMMUNICATE

The best preteen ministries have solid communication with the children's ministry leaders and middle school or junior high ministry leaders. These leaders need to be the preteen leader's best friends. All these leaders need to plan the transitions together so they go smoothly and students want to

> ### A LEADER'S THOUGHTS
>
> "Our junior high leader loved getting my students because it would infect the rest of his group. With preteen ministry, they're no longer scared to move up. Before, they were not ready to go and resisted it. It's a more natural transition, so it's easier for them."
>
> **—Craig Wilson,**
> *Children's Pastor*, California

make the moves. It's important to figure out how to make all the students feel comfortable.

The best preteen ministries transition students in and out intentionally. In the spring, they have meetings for parents of the incoming students to communicate goals of the ministry. They talk about both the regular activities and special events. A calendar of events is a great tool to distribute to parents. The best preteen ministries also let parents know how they can be involved. I haven't seen a ministry yet that had too many volunteers, so this is a perfect opportunity to encourage parents of incoming students to get involved.

BE INTENTIONAL

Louie, a leader at one of my favorite preteen ministries, is so intentional that he has a policy that the leader of the next older ministry fills in every time the leader of the younger ministry is away so students get to know their next leader. The leader of the older ministry also comes in and leads for two Sundays in May as well. The succeeding pastor leads at least 30% of the major events for the younger age level too. So the preteen leader has already led the children's ministry on numerous occasions and the students know him or her. This way, the students are familiar with their new leader and anxious to move up. Louie has a "kidnap breakfast" for the outgoing preteen students to transition and acclimate them to their new phase of ministry.

Joe, another great preteen leader, is equally intentional. He has a pizza party or similar event to welcome the fourth graders into the preteen ministry and a ceremonial farewell party for the outgoing sixth graders. The fourth graders come with their parents and learn about the ministry and have fun becoming familiar with their new surroundings. Parents find out that it's a safe, fun place for their preteens. For the farewell, Joe has the outgoing sixth graders do things such as sign a hubcap that hangs on the wall and add their pieces of chewed gum to the underside of a memorial table. The junior high leader is there also to welcome the students to the junior high ministry and get them pumped about being a part of it.

Katie, yet another great preteen leader, is intentional too. She does a cool thing called the Crossing for the outgoing students. The leaders of both the preteen and the junior high ministries are there. On one side of the room, the preteen volunteers say good-bye to the outgoing preteens. As the outgoing preteens cross to the other side, Katie hands each of them a cross and says something personal to them. On the other side, the junior high leader and students are waiting, cheering for the new incoming students. These new students are now officially junior high students and the junior high leader takes over.

One surprising thing I've seen is that preteens are more willing to move up to the middle school or junior high ministry if there is an intentional preteen ministry. The preteen ministry really helps prepare the students for the next step so it's not so scary for them.

If you need a reason to do preteen ministry, this is definitely a good one.

WELCOME AND GOOD-BYE TIPS

There are other cool things to do to welcome students to the preteen ministry. A kick-off event that includes food is always good. It can be done during your regular meeting time, before it, or after it—whatever works best. One idea you might want to try is to get the incoming students from their classrooms and escort them to the preteen room for the first time. This helps the incoming students feel safe and welcomed to the preteen ministry. I've heard about this being done with great pomp and ceremony. Including the parents or providing a special time to talk with parents is very important. You'll notice the differences between parents for whom this is their oldest child and parents with older children who have gone through this transition before.

Saying good-bye is as important as saying hello. Giving the outgoing students an appropriate send-off helps them leave with great memories and excitement for what comes next. Whatever can be done to help students move to the next level is important. None of us want any students to be lost during a transition. We want them to know that we know they are no longer children and, whether incoming or outgoing, they are important in Christ's kingdom.

HIT THE ROAD

Getting students out of the building

G etting students out of the building is important for lots of reasons. It helps students and volunteers see beyond their own ministry. I hear this from many of the leaders who come to SuperStart! events. At these events, students see preteens from lots of other churches, even friends they didn't know went to church. They get all excited seeing so many other students their own age in one place. They start to see that they're not the only preteens who go to church. They see other students who are excited about Jesus and the enthusiasm builds.

Of course, I think every preteen should come to a SuperStart! event, but that's not the only place to take students. There are camps, retreats, mystery trips, and planned evenings of fun. Some service projects will take preteens out of the building. All of these offer the opportunity for students to build stronger relationships with their leaders and other students, as well as to make decisions for Christ.

RELATIONSHIP BUILDING

Getting students out of the building is a perfect opportunity for relationship building. Students and leaders get to see each other in a unique environment and can interact on different levels. This helps both the students and the leaders get to know each other better, see each other as real people, and learn more about likes and dislikes, interests, and what's happening in each others' lives.

MAKING DECISIONS

There's something about getting students out of the building that steers them toward making decisions. Over and over I hear from preteen leaders that many of their students made decisions

CHECK THIS OUT:
PRETEEN BOYS READY TO GO PLACES

According to *The Nickelodeon/Youth Intelligence Tween Report: 3*, preteen boys have an astoundingly obsessive interest in cars and car culture. Preteen boys cited *Pimp My Ride, Car and Driver, Hot Rod*, and *Grand Theft Auto* as favorite TV, magazines, and video games.

The idea of going places without relying on a parent or sibling for transportation is highly appealing to preteens. In fact, qualitatively, when asked if they could be any age, preteens most frequently cite ages 16 and over, noting that they will be of driving age then.

www.trendcentral.com/trends/trendarticle.
asp?tcArticleId=1368

to follow Christ at our SuperStart! events. I also know that many students make decisions when their preteen ministry groups go on retreats. A different environment is powerful that way.

THERE'S MORE

There are other things that happen when students get out of the building. Many leaders feel that it's important for preteens to do something different, to experience something new. Getting out of your building may allow different students to shine. For example, students who have been rather shy may come out of their shells as they participate in projects or activities. Hitting the road may help some students discover that church and church events are really fun and they will start to invite their friends. Hitting the road may also help students realize they're getting to do something others at school don't get to do. As they talk about their fun experiences with friends at school, their friends may become interested in coming to church with them.

RETREATS

I know several preteen ministries that have retreats for their preteens. They often have separate retreats for boys and girls, which allows them to address the issues that relate to each gender and all those growing-up issues. Camps are also great for preteen students.

In his preteen ministry, Joe plans purity retreats, one for the boys and one for the girls. These retreats are not held at the church building. Sometimes the retreats are held at a retreat center, other times at someone's house. The boys' retreat is very ceremonial in nature. Dads or significant males are required to come with the boys. At the retreat they talk about manhood and what a godly man is like. They have a ceremony honoring the boys as they enter manhood. The dads are also given tools and resources that will help them talk with their boys once they return home.

The girls' retreat is for moms and their daughters. They have a ceremony where the girls are given teacups, signifying how precious they are and meant for a special purpose, not like a foam cup that is used and thrown away.

I've talked with a number of preteen leaders who also do separate retreats for boys and girls, helping parents and their preteens launch into the teen years with affirmation and direction. It's a great opportunity for students to make decisions for Christ. It's also a great opportunity for parents to hear the same message. I know that preteen leaders also use these retreats to help parents know some of the following: how to insure computer safety, how to identify the signs of depression, and even how to understand texting lingo. There are plenty of community organizations that are happy to offer resources in these areas and some might even provide great guest speakers. This is a huge gift to both the preteens and their parents because they're receiving tools for life that will help them with their relationships with God and with others.

MYSTERY NIGHTS

A number of the preteen ministries I know about have mystery nights every so often. The students show up and are taken to a mystery destination. And sometimes the mystery is that they stay at the building. When they do hit the road for fun, they might go to a movie, ice skating, bowling, or out for ice cream. Other times they might hit the road for a service project. When the students stay at the church building, they might have a wiener roast around a bonfire, play a game of sardines, or have a drive-in movie night with goofy cars they make from boxes. The students love to be surprised. They always have fun and look forward to the next outing. All of these outings don't have to include a gospel message. But do be sure all your events help students build relationships with each other, or with Jesus, or with both!

THINGS TO THINK ABOUT

It's important not to take away from experiences students will have in the middle school or junior high ministry. Students need to look forward to special things that will happen next. When we started the SuperStart! events, we listened to preteen leaders. These leaders placed limits on their activities so they weren't taking away from the junior high ministry. We found they were sensitive to the distance they would travel and the kinds of activities they would offer for their preteen students. A lot of their decisions had to do with safety. We intentionally plan SuperStart! events so students and their leaders will only have to travel a short distance to get to the events. We also try to find locations where students can stay at the host church or in nearby motels. And it's just two days, so there's only one night for the preteens to spend away from home. SuperStart! is a far different experience from Believe, our junior high events, and that's on purpose. We intentionally plan SuperStart! events to have a whole different feel—the events are held in church facilities and teach through characters rather than speakers. You'll probably want to incorporate some of these ideas into your ministry planning also.

It's critically important, especially for parents, to have your act together when you hit the road with preteens. This may be the first time that some students travel with a church group, other than for camps. Be sure you show you're on top of it. Tell parents where you're going, how you're getting there, who's driving, what you'll be doing, and how you're insuring their preteens' safety. For some parents this is a big deal because it is the first time they are letting their preteens go somewhere without them, so you have to show them you know what you're doing. For parents who are really worried, you might even want to let them come along.

Taking students of this age on the road, even if it's just across town, requires additional supervision and parental permission. For SuperStart! events, we require one adult for every five students.

Safety at this age is so important and adequate supervision helps provide that. High school and college students are good help, have lots of energy, and preteens love them. Parents are great sources of supervision and transportation too.

It may seem as though taking preteens out of the building is a lot of work, but remember the results are completely worth it. Students benefit from going places and so do the adults who come along. Relationships deepen, commitment levels grow, faith matures. Try one road trip and see what you think.

BEGINNINGS

Starting a preteen ministry

I f you already have a preteen ministry, you can skip this chapter. If you're just getting started, welcome to a fast growing area of ministry! It was a wild and crazy ride getting Super-Start! off the ground, but that's not the same as starting a preteen ministry in your church. That's another situation. So again, I got advice from people I know who have started awesome preteen ministries. Much of what's in this chapter is what I've learned from these preteen leaders.

Preteen ministry is such a blast. It's a critical ministry area for many reasons. It's the age when students are just starting to solidify their faith. It's the age when many students have a choice about whether to attend church; unfortunately, many opt out. When they opt out, so do their families. You can make a difference by giving preteens a reason to stay and deepen their faith. Go for it. You'll find huge blessings in the wild and crazy ride. I know I sure have.

THE VISION

There's a difference between being asked to start a preteen ministry in your church and you having the vision to start one. If someone in leadership at your church, such as the senior minister, has asked you to consider starting a preteen ministry, you need to listen to his rationale and expectations. One thing that's nice about this situation is that you know someone really wants this ministry and believes that you're the right person to lead it. In this case, you may first have to give this new idea some prayerful consideration and be convinced that this is a vital ministry. If you're the one with the vision, then you have a different job ahead of you. You may have to convince the leadership at your church of the need for a preteen ministry and your vision for it. What's nice about this situation is that you already have the vision and know the importance of a preteen ministry.

CHECK THIS OUT:
PRETEENS RATE YOUTH GROUPS

A poll posted on "It's My Life" (a Web site sponsored by PBS Kids Go!) asked preteens if they were in a youth group and how they felt about it. The response was overwhelmingly positive. Comments included:

"I luv my youth group!!"

"We do a lot of fun stuff, and it's interesting and cool at the same time. Like it actually makes me want to go."

"My youth minister preaches great sermons and we all feel very safe with each other! It's like being part of a big family."

Negative comments included problems with discipline, disorganization, and a lack of service opportunities.

Begin by clarifying your vision. Try to write down your vision in one sentence. Use it often. Tell everyone, even those you don't think will be interested. Talking about it will help you refine what you're thinking. Having a clear vision will also help in recruiting volunteers you never dreamed would be interested in preteen ministry. A clear vision will help build excitement too. Make sure you keep church leaders, parents, and students up-to-date on your thinking. Don't leave anyone out of the loop.

FIRST THINGS FIRST

The first step to take will be to figure out what your preteen ministry will be like. Answering the following questions might be helpful:

Why should we start a preteen ministry?

What is the goal of the ministry?

What are the two or three things that will define the ministry?

How can the ministry be described in one sentence?

There are certain people who should be on board and excited about the plans for the preteen ministry. Parents, church leaders, students, the elementary leader, and the junior high leader are all very important. I'd start by talking with the church leadership, the elementary leader, and the junior high leader. You may even be one of these leaders. Be sure you have a basic plan for the ministry and an idea of expenses. The plan doesn't have to be completely thought through, but having a basic plan will help when trying to cast a vision and explain the need for a preteen ministry. As soon as you have the support of these leaders, start talking with parents. We've already discussed how important it is to have their involvement, so you need to get parents on board as soon as possible.

Get advice from other preteen ministry leaders and read articles about preteen ministries in magazines or on the Web. There are a lot of questions you'll need to answer before getting started. Here are some to get you going:

What ages will be included?

When will we meet?

Where will we meet?

When will we start?

What should we do?

What will we be known for?

What do the preteens in our church want and need?

You may already know the answers to some of these questions. I'll try to help you think through some of the others.

Safety guidelines and policies are important to consider too. Just as in children's ministry, you need to do background checks on all volunteers, have permission forms for students who leave the church grounds, and have general policies in place for how things will run. You may be able to get some forms and policies from your elementary and junior high leaders. You can also get helps from other preteen leaders. There are plenty of people who will be willing to share with you, so don't hesitate to ask. Get lots of advice. Look at lots of policies and forms and then tailor them to fit your needs. When you're making your decisions on these matters, be sure you consult with your elementary and junior high leaders.

HAVE A TEAM

Starting a ministry is a lot of work, so enlist help. I work with a great team of people for our SuperStart! events. I'm so much more creative and effective because of them. It's a great asset to have a team. Find some people who are as passionate about preteens as you. It's best to have people with a variety of gifts on your team too. If you're not administrative-minded, then find those who are and ask them to join the team. If you're not artistic, then find those who are and ask them to join the team. You'll also need some who are musical, some who are teachers, and some who are good recruiters. At first, you may be the one who fills several of these roles. Similar to small-group ratio guidelines, you'll want between four to eight individuals on your team.

WHAT AGES?

If you're not sure about what ages to include, preteen ministry is usually just for two years, either fourth and fifth grades or fifth and sixth grades. It's generally determined by the school districts around you. Look at how the schools are organized. If there are middle schools, then you will most likely want to have fourth and fifth graders. If there are junior high schools, then you will most likely want to have fifth and sixth graders. There's also a whole range of other organizations in schools, so look around and see what students are experiencing. Choose what's best for your students.

A preteen ministry must be age appropriate from the very beginning. It has to look preteen and sound preteen. Preteen ministry is different from elementary ministry. The worship is more mature and the songs are more complex. The students are beginning to think a little more and ask deeper questions.

They're far more relational and friends are important to them. They need more freedom and choice. Preteen ministry is also different from junior high ministry. Preteens aren't as sure of themselves as junior high students. They're just beginning to think abstractly. Preteens need more structure and instruction during a service or class. The boys are still pretty silly. Parents expect more safety precautions with preteens than they do with junior high students.

A LEADER'S THOUGHTS

"Make sure that your preteen ministry is age appropriate from the beginning. By design, our preteen ministry has the cool feel of being similar to a middle school youth group, but it also has the safety and teaching principles that an elementary ministry might have. Our preteen ministry has a different feel to it than children's ministry."

—Louie Murillo,
Family Life Minister, Texas

WHEN AND WHERE?

If you want to find a place and time to meet, your best option is to talk with the leaders of the elementary and junior high ministries at your church. You may have to be creative. I know a lot of preteen ministries that share space with either the elementary ministry or the middle school/junior high ministry. One idea many ministries use is when either the elementary group or the middle school group is in its large-group time, the preteen ministry is having its small-group time. Then they trade places. This is just one more reason why working closely with the other age-level leaders is very important.

You can start your preteen ministry any time. I've seen great ministries launch at almost any time of the year. But don't start before you're ready. Take time to adequately plan and inform. Take time to recruit and train. Take time to prepare a great launch with plenty of help from parents and other volunteers. As much as possible, get everything in place. Then start telling everyone what you're going to do—and tell them again. But since nothing will ever be perfect, don't wait until you think things are perfect, or you may never start.

DO WHAT?

You don't need to start big. Whatever you do, the preteens will be grateful. So will the parents. Whatever you do, do it with excellence. Size is not as important as quality. Don't wait until you have 65 students and don't know what to do with them. Start now by being intentional with the students you have. If you start with five students, when you have ten, you'll have doubled your ministry. That's pretty good!

If you need some help deciding what to do in your new preteen ministry, talking with preteens and their parents is best. Listen to their wants, needs, and concerns. Look at other preteen ministries too. There are also great preteen blogs where you can get good advice about quality preteen ministries. If you start asking around, you'll find plenty of help. I know I've said this many times before, but I'm going to say it again: Be sure to know what is best for your individual students and ministry. You're not supposed to be like any other ministry. Use ideas from other ministries; but don't worry about being just like them.

You might want to start with a Sunday morning class, a Wednesday evening group, or

A LEADER'S THOUGHTS

"Call it the Preteen Ministry and give it a name. They love the word because it makes them feel a little more grown up. Use it as much as you can. It gives them something of their very own."

—Katie Gerber,
Preteen Ministry Associate,
Indiana

monthly gatherings. They're all great ways to start. Prioritize the things you want to do. Start with one and add another when you're ready and have the help. Be realistic with your time, expectations, and budget. You know what you and your team can do.

A PRETEEN ENVIRONMENT

Branding a preteen ministry gives it an identity and helps create an environment. Environment is really important in preteen ministry. It sets the tone and gives the students something to relate to. Every year we create a specific environment for SuperStart! events. We do it through our characters, the set, and the music. The way you set up your preteen ministry area is part of the environment.

The name of your ministry influences the environment too. Choosing things such as a name and a logo is easier to do by yourself, but including parents and students gets them even more more involved and invested in the ministry. When you are starting a ministry, involving students and parents is crucial. When parents and students are involved, things can take interesting turns, so be prepared to set boundaries and exercise veto power. Once you have a name and logo, plaster them everywhere. Decorate your space as much as you're allowed. Interested parents will help with this.

Got a name, a place, a plan, and a team? Then gather your preteens and get going!

TRUE
CONFESSIONS

Mistakes and sticky situations to avoid

Any time you're in ministry, you're going to make some mistakes and run into some sticky situations. At least I hope I'm not the only one who's messed up or encountered sticky situations. I never try to make mistakes, but they do happen. Sometimes I know right away that I've caused or contributed to a sticky situation. Other times someone has to take me aside and point it out. A few of my friends who are great preteen leaders have helped me by confessing some of their own mistakes and sticky situations to help me avoid the same pitfalls. The following are some mistakes and sticky situations to avoid, but they're not an exhaustive list. I thought I'd be a friend and share this information in hopes of helping you some time.

ALWAYS ENCOURAGE

I've found that I have to be careful not to embarrass a student. At SuperStart! events and at church, preteens love to volunteer to

CHECK THIS OUT:
10 TIPS TO AVOID MISTAKES

1. Count heads often.
2. Always assume the best of everyone.
3. When anyone says "everyone," don't believe it.
4. Always bring a nurse on trips, to camps, etc.
5. Never say never.
6. Remember that God's not surprised by anything.
7. Don't hide anything.
8. Take plastic grocery bags wherever you go; they're as versatile as duct tape.
9. Just be you.
10. If something goes wrong, just take the blame whether it's yours or not.

be in front of the rest of the students and say or do something. When they say something odd or do something strange that wasn't meant to be funny, I have to remember to not laugh at or embarrass them. There's a fine line I don't want to cross between laughing with students and making fun of them. If I think I've accidentally crossed the line, I do my best to include myself in what the students are saying or doing so they're not alone. I always try to encourage students and send them away feeling good, no matter what they've said or not said.

BE AGE APPROPRIATE

When I'm at SuperStart! events or with the boys in my small group at church, I want to avoid the mistake of treating them too old or too young. Sometimes I'm amazed at what preteens know, and sometimes I'm surprised by what they don't know yet. I find a pretty big gap even among the boys in my small group, let alone all the students in a large-group setting.

Some students may have already been exposed to alcohol or sex issues because they have older siblings or they live in a household that encourages discussion about these issues. Other preteens may not have a clue about these issues and their parents don't want them to be exposed to those things yet. It's a tough call on what you should and shouldn't be talking about with students this age.

You'll also find that every group of students is different. If I'm not sure about certain topics, I'll check with some parents who I know and trust. They usually give me some pretty good advice.

> ### A LEADER'S THOUGHTS
>
> "Sometimes the info you see on preteens is a little unrealistic. The average preteen may not be dealing with alcohol use, sex, drugs, etc. It's just not realistic. I'd rather have them focus on the basics so they'll know how to make decisions when they do face these things."
>
> **—Craig Wilson,**
> *Children's Pastor*, California

PROOF EVERYTHING

An easy mistake to make is to send out information that isn't complete or correct. I've found that I always need to have someone proof everything before it's sent out because I can leave out the most obvious information. Since I've probably already spent a lot of time thinking about upcoming events, I just don't check the details like I should. Have someone else look at letters, e-mails, and postcards before you send them out. It'll save you tons of time and frustration later.

HAVE PROPER EXPECTATIONS

Another easy mistake to make is to expect students to get serious right after doing something crazy or silly. I need to plan activities that compliment each other or build on each other. If I plan a crazy, high-energy activity, I probably need to follow that with an activity a little less active, and then go on to a quiet or more serious activity. Preteens usually can't be wild and crazy one minute and then be suddenly super serious the next. I guess they're pretty much like me.

Don't expect students to remember or commit to events that are planned very far in the future. A long-term commitment to preteens is sometimes only one or two days from now. So if you're planning something for next month or even next weekend, plan on reminding them several times. Send postcards or e-mails to their parents reminding them too. One of the worst things you can do is to spend lots of time and energy planning something and then have only a few students show up simply because they weren't reminded to come.

USE TECHNOLOGY WISELY

Technology is a great tool, but I've also experienced when it can be a great hindrance. If I'm going to use computers, CD and DVD players, and projection equipment in preteen ministry, someone has to make sure that it's all working and someone has to be running it besides me or whoever the leader is. If something goes wrong with the technology, I don't want to be the one to go mess with it. It's up to me to keep the students involved and participating while someone else solves the technology problem. If I get involved in the technology, I lose the students. I also make sure to have a back-up plan when it comes to using technology. If the technology fails, what will I do instead? I have to be able to keep going with the lesson, whether or not the PowerPoint or DVD works.

RECRUIT AND EMPOWER A TEAM

One of the preteen leaders I respect the most is Louie. He's given me plenty of wise advice over the years. Louie tells of one sticky situation that could have been avoided if he had recruited the right amount of volunteers and empowered them. The church Louie serves with started a preteen ministry because no one in their community was addressing that need. Louie only recruited and staffed for the number of students who were currently in that age group. Two weeks after the launch of the preteen ministry, there were so many more preteens than anticipated that he had to do massive recruiting. Having too much help is always better than not having enough. Recruiting ahead of time makes everything work better and avoids a lot of sticky situations that can result from not having enough volunteers.

Besides recruiting a team, Louie tells me that the team has to be empowered. Lots of my other friends in ministry would second this. Volunteers sign up to help, so be sure to put them to work. Give volunteers well-defined jobs with clear expectations, train them, and then turn them loose to serve. And be sure to provide encouragement and any additional information and training along the way. If I don't give volunteers the opportunity to serve, I rob them of the joy that comes from serving. And that's not fair.

OVERPLAN AND PRACTICE

Katie, another preteen leader I respect, tells me to overplan. She makes sure she has plans B and C in place in case plan A doesn't work. When Katie plans an outside event, she also has an alternate inside event planned in case it rains. She has alternate plans ready for times when the adult program runs long, one or more of the volunteers don't show, she gets through the lesson more quickly than she thought she would, or a student vomits. She obviously can't plan for every possibility, but the more she's thought through the sticky situations that can arise, the more likely she'll know what to do in other sticky situations.

Another thing Katie tells me is to practice. She illustrates her point with this story: "I can't tell you how many times I have gotten in trouble because I didn't go over what I was going to say before I started talking. One time I did a communion meditation. I started by talking about the movie *Chronicles of Narnia,* then talked about being scared of rats, and finished by talking about Jesus dying on a cross. There's probably some very talented person out there who could've made those transitions beautifully, but mine was way off the charts. My point—preteens are so smart that they'll know when you are not prepared."

I know from SuperStart! events that Katie's advice to practice is totally true. We spend weeks preparing our events and we also practice in between event weekends, tweaking things because of what we've learned.

DO WHAT YOU SAY

Joe tells me to do what I say. If Joe says he's going to do something, he's gotta do it. If he tells the students he's going to pray for them, he'd better do it. If he's going to bring pizza next week, there'd better be pizza. And if he says he's not going to do something, then he can't do it. For example, if Joe says he's not going to let any students help with lights or sound, then he can't bend the rule for his favorite student next month. If he says he's not going to let fourth graders come to a certain event, he can't let any of them come, even if an older student wants to bring a fourth grade friend who wants to hear about Jesus.

LEARN FROM MISTAKES

Craig, another great preteen leader, tells me to keep the proper balance between outreach and service. He grew a fantastic preteen ministry based on service. Then when the ministry started growing, the leaders leaned more toward outreach to keep new students coming and slacked off on the service aspect. Looking back, Craig says they'd have been better off keeping the proper balance of service along with the outreach.

The wisest advice from Craig, though, is to not be afraid to make mistakes. It takes a pioneering spirit to launch and run a preteen ministry. Don't be afraid to learn as you go. Try new things and don't be afraid. If something didn't work like you anticipated, well, try something different. It's not the end of the world. Preteens are pretty forgiving if you're really trying to minister to them.

A lot of preteen leaders tell me they wish they would have involved parents more from the beginning. Often, as preteen ministries are getting started, parents can seem threatening, so leaders avoid involving them. Parents, as was discussed in Chapter Seven, are the best asset you can have in preteen ministry.

DO WHAT GOD CALLED YOU TO DO

One thing I've seen is that some preteen leaders try to be someone they're not. It's so important to understand that God created each of us with different personalities and different gifts. My personality and gifts are not the same as yours. I'm gifted to talk a certain way and to do certain things. You're gifted to do other things just as important, probably more so. So do what God needs you to do. And I'll do what God's called me to do. In that way, many more preteens will be reached for Christ.

None of the mistakes we've described are lethal. None are going to mar your ministry forever. All are forgivable. One thing is for sure: we all make mistakes. No matter how hard we try, we just won't be perfect. Neither will our volunteers or students. We're all in the same boat. None of our mistakes take God by surprise. Do your best and your students, volunteers, parents, and senior pastor will be forgiving. God's grace is always available. Your humanness will allow you to minister authentically and relate to students who struggle with making mistakes too.

Ministering to these students is a fun ride. My prayer is that you will be blessed as you minister to preteens. I know I have been!

The event for preteens is here! And it's called

SuperStart!

www.ciy.com/superstart

SuperStart! travels nationally for weekend events in the spring and fall. Find a location near you by visiting our web site, www.ciy.com/superstart

ciy An Event Just For Preteens From Christ In Youth